# Positive Brain Habits

## Unleashing the Power of Your Mind

By 

## Robert Gildon

# TABLE OF CONTENTS

# Introduction

We frequently find ourselves looking for ways to enhance our general well-being and happiness in today's fast-paced environment. What if the secret to a happy existence lay within the complex operations of our brains? Recent scientific studies have illuminated the fascinating subject of healthy brain habits and their enormous effects on both our productivity and mental health. The process of achieving control over one's ideas, emotions, and behaviors is referred to as mastering the mind.

It entails comprehending how the mind functions, spotting harmful thought patterns, developing constructive thinking patterns, and utilizing the power of our thoughts. *To successfully navigate through life's problems and accomplish personal progress, increasing self-awareness, emotional intelligence, and cognitive abilities.*

Being able to control one's thoughts helps people control their emotions. They can comprehend and control their emotional reactions, which improves their emotional stability and well-being.

This ability aids *in decision-making, relationship improvement, and stress reduction*. It is essential for preserving mental wellness. *It entails identifying negative thought habits, confronting illogical assumptions, and fostering optimistic thinking. People can conquer anxiety*, depression, and other mental health issues by becoming mind masters. **People who have mastered their minds can keep their attention on their objectives and tasks.** *Distractions are reduced, concentration is improved, and overall productivity is raised.* People who are focused and have a clear head can accomplish more in less time. Additionally, it increases resilience and adaptability under pressure. It gives people the tools they need to recover from setbacks, take lessons from mistakes, and adapt to novel circumstances. This ability enables people to overcome obstacles and keep an optimistic view amid trying circumstances. The promotion of self-awareness that comes from mind control is essential for personal development. It aids people in comprehending their assets, liabilities, values, and convictions. Self-awareness enables people to match their behavior with their values and aspirations, resulting in a more fulfilling and meaningful existence. The most effective weapon we have at our disposal for achieving success at all levels in life is our thinking.

Our thoughts affect our physical and mental health as well as who we are today and who we will become in the future. We are only now starting to fully understand and use the power of the mind.

# Chapter 1

# The Power of the Mind

## *Understanding Your Brain's Potential

Throughout history, scientists, philosophers, and inquisitive minds have been enthralled by the human brain, an incredibly intricate and amazing organ. The immense potential that every one of us possesses is revealed as we dive more into the field of neurology. Our brains can significantly alter our world and improve the quality of our lives, from cognitive functions to creative thinking.

Understanding the concept of neuroplasticity is the first step in understanding the potential of our brains. The days when we thought the brain was a static structure incapable of modification or adaptation are long gone. We have a remarkable capacity for learning, growth, and transformation thanks to neuroplasticity, the brain's capability to rearrange and generate new neural connections.

Our thinking, reasoning, and problem-solving abilities are shaped by a wide spectrum of cognitive abilities. Our brains can improve these cognitive skills and maximize our mental performance, from memory and attention to language and decision-making. *We may increase focus, memory retention, and overall cognitive performance by using a variety of strategies, such as brain-training exercises, meditation, and healthy eating.* Creativity and innovation are frequently regarded as traits of the human intellect, and everyone has the capacity for creative thought. *Divergent thinking exercises, brainstorming, and exposure to new situations can all boost our brain's creative areas,* allowing us to come up with original ideas and answers.

Our brains serve as the focal point for both our intellectual and emotional experiences. Success in both the personal and professional spheres depends heavily on emotional intelligence, or the capacity to recognize and control emotions.

Our emotional intelligence can be improved by methods like mindfulness, self-reflection, and empathy training, which can help our brains reach their full potential.

It is crucial to place a high priority on brain health and lifespan if we are to fully utilize the potential of our brains. We may maintain healthy brain function and prevent cognitive decline by making lifestyle decisions including regular exercise, a balanced diet, good sleep habits, and mental stimulation. By taking care of our brains, we build a space where we can flourish *academically, creatively, and emotionally,* maximizing the potential of our brains throughout our lives.

## *Habits and Their Effects on Our Lives

***Conscious and unconsciously*** formed habits are crucial in determining how our lives turn out. These entrenched habits control our behavior from the moment we wake up until we lay our heads down at night. Whether we are aware of it or not, our habits shape who we are and have a significant impact on our

**general success, happiness, and well-being.** Essentially, routines or behaviors that we repeatedly engage in without realizing it are called habits. They may cover a range of facets of our existence, such as our **emotional, mental, and physical routines**. As our brains attempt to become more efficient by automating processes, habits are frequently developed through repetition.

Not all habits are helpful, though; some can be harmful and prevent us from attaining our full potential. We must first comprehend the idea of the habit loop to comprehend the effects of habits.

*(The cue, the routine, and the reward)* are the three phases of the habit loop. The habit is started by a cue, followed by a routine, which includes the action itself, and a reward, which reinforces the habit. Recognizing this cycle allows us to

examine and improve our habits to promote growth. Positive habits are the cornerstone of success and personal development. *They have the power to influence our relationships, mental health, physical healthcare,* and *career success.* For instance, regular exercise not only increases our physical health but also our **cognitive function and mood**. Similarly to this, developing a habit of lifelong learning equips us to adapt to a world that is changing quickly by increasing our knowledge and broadening our viewpoints.

**(*Removing Bad Habits*)**

On the other hand, bad habits might impede our development and prevent us from reaching our full potential. Whether it's smoking, spending too much time on screens, or procrastinating, these behaviors are bad for our health, productivity, and general well-being. It takes self-awareness, discipline, and a strong desire to change to break away from bad behaviors. We can gradually remove ourselves from harmful behaviors by substituting healthy alternatives for the triggers and underlying factors that lead to them.

**(The Power of Stacking Habits)**

Habit stacking is a powerful method for modifying habits. Using the power of association to bring about long-lasting change, this technique entails connecting a new habit to an already-formed one. We can make it simpler to develop and sustain new habits by tying a desired behavior to an existing routine. For instance, if your objective is to read more, you can combine it with your morning coffee to establish a ritual that will help you read more. While forming new habits and breaking old ones might be difficult, consistency and effort are the keys to long-lasting transformation. Rewiring our minds and changing deeply ingrained tendencies require time and effort.

The process of changing our habits requires several different steps, including cultivating a supportive *environment requesting* accountability from others, and engaging in self-compassion exercises. Our behaviors make up the entirety of our life. We can actively control our future by realizing the power of habits and comprehending the habit loop.

Our everyday decisions have a significant impact on our success, happiness, and well-being, whether it's forming healthy habits for personal development or letting go of unhelpful patterns. We can realize our full potential and lead lives of meaning and fulfillment by accepting the possibility of change and developing an attitude of continual improvement. Never forget that we can change our tale, one behavior at a time.

# Chapter 2

## The Neuroscience of Habit Formation

***The Secret  Of Self-Awareness**

It's simple to get caught up in the commotion of daily life in the fast-paced and complex world we live in without pausing to take stock of who we are. *But the basis of personal development and fulfillment is self-awareness.*

The ability to unbiasedly examine and comprehend oneself is the essence of self-awareness. It entails being aware of our thoughts, feelings, and behaviors without passing judgment or taking offense.

*The practice of mindfulness through meditation and other mindfulness-based exercises teaches us to be conscious of our thoughts, feelings, and physical sensations in the present momen*t. This technique fosters a non-judgmental and inquisitive attitude toward our inner experiences, which heightens self-awareness.

Writing down our *thoughts, emotions, and experiences regularly can be a highly effective technique for self-reflection.* We can learn more about our routines, triggers, and goals through journaling. For self-expression and self-discovery, it offers a secure environment. By coordinating our behavior with our ideals and beliefs, self-awareness helps us live genuinely. Our sense of fulfillment and purpose in life increases as we become more aware of our passions, desires, and purposes.

Being self-aware allows us to recognize and comprehend our emotions, which gives us the power to manage them successfully. We become more responsive and less reactive, which helps us make better judgments and enhance our general well-being.

Empathy and compassion for others are fostered by self-awareness, which improves our capacity to comprehend their viewpoints and resolve differences amicably. A crucial talent for the workplace is self-awareness. It enables us to identify our assets and liabilities, adjust to various work settings, and make the most of our particular skills. Make time each day for introspection and self-reflection. Inquire deeply about your beliefs, objectives, dreams, and anxieties by asking yourself probing questions.

Become deeply introspective to better understand your drives, aspirations, and reasons for acting as you do. It takes persistence, dedication, and practice to develop self-awareness, which is a lifelong process. Our true potential can be unlocked and we can live a more genuine and fulfilling life by making time for introspection and self-reflection.

## *The Influence of Intention

The power of the human mind to alter reality is truly amazing. We can make use of this innate potential by using the power of intention to make our goals come true and rewrite the course of our lives. *Our dreams are ignited and propelled toward fulfillment by intention, which serves as a catalyst.*

The intention is fundamentally the conscious process of guiding our thoughts, feelings, and deeds toward a

**specific goal.** It transcends wishful thinking and *straightforward goal-setting.* The intention is a conscious decision that unites our internal aspirations with our outward behaviors, resulting in a potent synergy that moves us ahead. Science has examined and accepted the idea of intention; disciplines like quantum physics and neurobiology have done so.

These fields of study give light on the ways that purpose can affect the physical world. Personal development and self-discovery are sparked by intention. By establishing clear intentions, we may define our goals and plot a path to bettering ourselves. Intention has the power to affect not just the lives of individuals but also the entire community. A group's collective energy multiplies its power when members come together with a common goal. The intention is not immune to difficulties and failures.

To effectively use the power of intention, it's important to know how to overcome these challenges and build resilience. The practice of intention is a way of life, not a one-time event.

# Chapter 3

## Cultivating Positive Thought Patterns

### *Combating Self-Negative Talk

The difficulty of negative self-talk has become all too frequent for many people. Our self-esteem, confidence, and general well-being are all hampered by critical and self-deprecating ideas, which are referred to as negative self-talk. But with the correct attitude and techniques, we may discover how to break free from this negative habit and develop a more uplifting and inspiring inner conversation.

**Our internalized ideas, prior experiences, societal expectations, or comparisons to others are common causes of negative self-talk.** The first step in changing this tendency is realizing the effects of negative self-talk. Recognize that you can confront and reframe your negative beliefs and that your inner voice might not always be fair or true. Start by focusing on your thoughts and feelings as they arise during the day. **Keep an eye out for the times when you start talking badly to yourself and look for any patterns or triggers.** Challenge your negative self-talk habits when you've identified them using logic supported by evidence. Consider whether these unfavorable ideas are purely self-imposed restrictions or whether there is any actual evidence to back them up.

Negative ideas frequently stem from presumptions, misperceptions, or irrational concerns. Change them for more practical and empowering ones. Offer yourself the same sympathy and support you would extend to a close friend rather than criticizing yourself for perceived defects or mistakes. Accept your flaws and keep in mind *that everyone experiences difficulties and makes mistakes.* Exercise self-care and partake in activities that are good for your body, soul, and mind. *Spend Time with Positive People Look for uplifting reading, inspirational sayings, or affirmations in the positive.* It gets simpler to stop negative self-talk the more positive influences you expose yourself to.

When we compare ourselves to others or have unrealistic expectations for ourselves, negative self-talk frequently results. Instead, make attainable goals that reflect your values and interests. It can be difficult to stop negative self-talk, so it's acceptable to ask for help. Speak with dependable relatives, friends, or experts who can offer advice, inspiration, and perspective. Consider therapy or counseling as a useful tool to investigate more profound concerns and create workable coping mechanisms.

# Chapter 4

## The Magic of Affirmations

## *Making Powerful Affirmations

To overcome obstacles and accomplish our goals in today's fast-paced, cutthroat environment, it is essential to establish a positive mindset. Affirmations are a potent tool for encouraging a positive outlook. Positive sentences that we repeat to ourselves are called affirmations. These remarks have an intentional impact on our ideas, beliefs, and ultimately, our behaviors. Affirmations may be transformative when they are written well because they can help us get over self-doubt, build confidence, and actualize the life we want. Our neurological pathways and cognitive processes are changed by affirmations.

They work best when combined with other techniques for personal development like goal-setting, visualization, and action planning. *Focusing on the positive is the first step in creating powerful affirmations.* Affirmations should focus on what we want to become or achieve rather than on what we lack or want to improve. *Rephrase statements like, "I embrace challenges and learn from every experience," rather than "I am not afraid of failure." This change in viewpoint strengthens the growth mentality and creates the conditions for achievement and personal development.*

Affirmations work best when they are clear, concise, and focused on what you want. Vague statements lack focus and may not have a powerful emotional impact on you. Consider tailoring your affirmation to reflect your definition of success rather than just saying, "I want to be successful," for example.

It might be more powerful to say, *"I am confidently building my successful career as a respected leader in my field."*Always utilize the present tense and positive language while writing affirmations.

Your subconscious mind will be informed that your ideal world already exists if you affirm the present. **Avoid using terms** *like "not" or "don't"* since they emphasize the drawbacks you're trying to get rid of. Saying, *"I am not frightened of public speaking,"* for instance, may be rephrased as, *"I am a confident and dynamic speaker who captivates audiences with my words.*

Always be genuine and personal in your affirmations. Personalization is necessary when creating powerful affirmations. **Make sure your statements reflect your basic beliefs, interests, and goals.** Think about the things that honestly speak to you and the things that you sincerely want to create in your life. **Affirmations may be strong motivators that spark your inner drive and propel your forward movement when they are genuine and in line with who**

**you are.** The most crucial thing is consistency while using affirmations. Schedule a certain time each day to practice your affirmations. They can be incorporated into your daily routine, your bedtime ritual, or even when you're feeling anxious or doubtful.

Your affirmations will become more deeply buried in your subconscious mind as you repeat them, altering your thoughts and behavior. Affirmations should be infused with emotions to increase their potency. Your affirmations can spur change when you have a strong emotional connection to them. Visualize the feelings that come with reaching your objectives and include them in your comments.

## *Including Affirmations in Everyday Life

Affirmations are a potent technique that has become very popular. Affirmations can help us rewire our cognitive processes, increase our self-esteem, and cultivate a positive mindset. *Positive affirmations are repeated to oneself repeatedly, whether consciously or unconsciously, to change our ideas and actions.* They act as potent reminders of our potential, ideals, and goals. The secret to their success is their capacity to transform unfavorable self-talk into motivating ideas. Affirmations, according to research, can boost motivation, boost self-esteem, and reduce stress.

Choose personal affirmations that are consistent with your objectives and desires to start incorporating them into your daily life. Spend some time reflecting on your life and the areas where you would like to make improvements.

*These spheres may encompass personal development, relationships, career, health, and self-assurance. Create precise,* uplifting affirmations that are in line with your principles. Affirmations work best when they are consistent. You may take full use of this potent instrument if you establish a daily practice. As part of your daily routine, recite affirmations to get your day off to a good start. As you visualize the desired results, repeat your affirmations aloud or silently. Setting a good example for the day ahead, this practice. In front of a mirror, take a few steps back, gaze into your eyes, and firmly state your affirmations.

With the help of this strategy, your affirmations will have a stronger emotional connection, increasing their potency. Use routine tasks as reminders to say affirmations. You might say your affirmations out loud or through affirming podcasts or playlists while exercising, driving, doing the dishes, or any other activity. When first incorporating affirmations into daily life, it's typical to run against resistance or doubt. Your progress could be hampered by negative self-talk or a lack of conviction. Follow these tactics to get through these **challenges**: Even if you don't notice any improvements right away, continue using affirmations every day **(consistency)**. Repetition builds new neural connections that progressively change your perspective.

**(Emotional Connection)** Recite affirmations while being emotionally present. Your remarks might have a good effect on your life if you sincerely believe they are true.

*(Affirmations for Difficult Times)* Use affirmations to boost your confidence and inspire you when things are tough. You can use them to combat self-doubt and take its place with assurance.

Accountability and Assistance With a spouse, friend, or support group you can trust, discuss your affirmation journey. You can maintain your dedication and motivation by receiving support and accountability.

## Conclusion:

## Unleashing Your Inner Power

The tremendous potential and resources that each person possesses are what is meant by "unleashing the power within." It entails identifying and utilizing our inner resources to make positive changes in our lives and the world we live in. When we unleash the power within, we realize our potential and unearth the skills that frequently go unused or unused.

It necessitates self-awareness, tenacity, and readiness to stretch ourselves. *We can go through constraints, and scale walls, and produce remarkable outcomes by doing this.* A journey of personal development and transformation leads to unleashing the power within. It entails pushing ourselves to new limits, making big plans, and working consistently to achieve them. It necessitates adopting a positive outlook, viewing setbacks as teaching moments, and persevering in the face of difficulty.

We can find our secret abilities, passions, and drives by reflecting on ourselves, discovering who we are, and improving ourselves. We can learn more about who we are, what we value, and what our life's work is. This process enables us to live more purposeful lives by enabling us to make conscious decisions, align our behaviors with our true selves, and live more authentic lives.

Unleashing the force within is also a group effort; it doesn't just affect the person. We motivate and empower those around us as we realize our potential. By fostering positivity and causing a chain reaction of change in our neighborhoods and society as a whole, we become agents of change. discovering our ability to control our destiny and affect change in the world is the essence of discovering our power within. It is a call to action that exhorts us to realize our full potential, fervently pursue our goals and make a positive difference in the world for the benefit of the future. By releasing the power within, we can live genuinely amazing lives and leave a lasting legacy for future generations.